THE POCKET COACH

JAE ELLARD

WHAT IS A COACH AND
WHY DO I WANT ONE IN MY POCKET?

The purpose of a coach is to empower you to do better than you are currently doing at something.

THAT "SOMETHING" COULD BE ANYTHING.

You can be coached in sports, cooking, singing, acting, presenting, reading financials, or on bigger issues like parenting, relationships, your health, or your career.

One thing coaches have in common, regardless of what they are coaching you on, is that they are there to help **YOU** see **YOUR** skill and ability in a new way. They are there to **EMPOWER YOU** to be the best you can be at whatever it is you want to be.

When it comes to sports or learning a specific skill, working with a coach who has expertise in that area will go a long way to help you improve your skills.

It's a different story when it comes to areas like relationships, health, and career, because there is only one expert in this area and **THE EXPERT IS YOU.**

What makes people who coach others in these areas successful is the simple fact **THEY ARE EXPERTS AT ASKING QUESTIONS,** questions that generate a new perspective.

Coaches ask **PROVOCATIVE** questions, **POWERFUL** questions, and sometimes very **OBVIOUS** questions.

Coaches ask questions that **GIVE YOU PAUSE.**

You might want to avoid answering them because you know THE ANSWER YOU COME UP WITH IS GOING TO ROCK YOUR WORLD.

The most amazing part about this type of coaching is that **YOU ARE THE ONLY ONE WHO HAS THE ANSWERS TO THESE QUESTIONS.**

THERE IS NO RIGHT OR WRONG ANSWER — THERE IS JUST THE ANSWER.

THE COACH IN YOUR POCKET IS YOU.

THE REALITY IS
SOME DAYS ROCK,
SOME DAYS ARE SO-SO, AND
SOME DAYS REALLY SUCK.

For the days that really suck, there are questions to help make it suck less, questions to get you unstuck and help you be the best you can be... at whatever it is you are trying to be.

YOU'RE NO FOOL.

You know when you're facing a challenge you need to work through, when you have a problem you need to solve, or when there's a person in your life driving you nuts. You know when you're avoiding doing or saying something, just like you know when you're running away from accepting a change.

The hard part is knowing **WHAT TO DO NEXT**.

Many times the answer of "what to do next" comes from being asked the right question.

Being asked the right question can clear the mind chatter, break down "the story" you've created, and unlock the simple truth.

Most times **IT DOESN'T REALLY MATTER WHO** is asking the questions, but rather that **THE RIGHT QUESTIONS ARE BEING ASKED.**

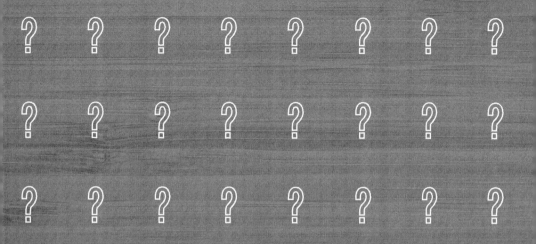

WHY WAIT FOR SOMEONE TO ASK YOU THE QUESTIONS?

WHY NOT ASK THE QUESTIONS OF YOURSELF?

There are proven questions that can move you forward, shake you free, shake you up, or release you from the past.

Something magical about these questions is that you can ask the same question and get a completely different answer each time you ask it.

Because life is like that — THINGS CHANGE AND ALL SITUATIONS, SCENARIOS, AND PEOPLE ARE DIFFERENT AND EVER EVOLVING.

There are themes and patterns in life. These themes and patterns are linked to common feelings most people share about their current and future state of being, regardless of gender, ethnicity, or social or economic status.

COMMON STATES OF BEING PEOPLE EXPERIENCE:

☑ My life sucks

☑ I'm confused and feel blocked

☑ I'm scared to death of what's next

☑ I want to feel good

☑ I feel all alone

☑ Everyone else has gone crazy

☑ I can't see my future

When you experience one of these states, reach into your pocket and pull yourself out.

By asking questions and receiving answers you will empower yourself to create a future that is different from your past.

MY LIFE SUCKS

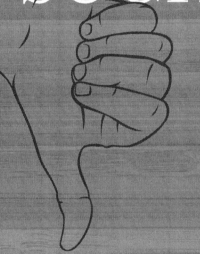

REALLY?

Does your life really, truly suck?

It might, and that's okay if that's where you are.

Perhaps you're going through a big change and life has you turned all about. Or maybe you're depressed because things are not going well and you see no end in sight.

Despair not, there is freedom in your answers. Answer one of the following questions or perhaps two or three or even all of them if that's what feels right.

WHAT DO YOU WANT RIGHT NOW THAT

YOU DON'T HAVE?

WHY ARE YOU DOING WHAT YOU ARE DOING?

HOW DOES THIS SERVE YOU?

WHAT ARE YOU TOLERATING?

WHAT CONVERSATIONS ARE YOU NOT HAVING

WITH YOURSELF?

WHAT IS THE LIE YOU ARE LIVING?

WHEN IS IT ENOUGH?

BE OPEN TO YOUR ANSWERS

I'M CONFUSED AND FEEL BLOCKED

Most everyone alive can identify with feeling confused or blocked at one time or another. It's a helpless feeling. Being in this space is mental paralysis, where you have no earthly idea of where to go next. Sure, you see options, you know you have choices, but for some reason nothing is coming together. You don't know which direction to move, so you sit. You remain still as the frustration and discontent grows and your mind is in overdrive trying to force action, any action, but none will come.

Ease up on yourself, sit back, and consider things anew. Try taking the 10,000-foot approach, get out of the weeds, and look at the big picture. Sometimes solving the right problem is more than half of the solution.

WHAT CONCERNS YOU THE MOST?

WHAT OPPORTUNITY ARE YOU WASTING RIGHT NOW?

WHAT CAN YOU DO ABOUT IT?

WHERE IS YOUR ATTENTION MOST OF THE TIME?

WHERE DO YOU LIMIT YOURSELF?

WHERE ARE YOU TOO COMFORTABLE?

WHAT IS LACKING OR MISSING THAT YOU NEED TO

MOVE FORWARD?

I'M CONFUSED
AND FEEL BLOCKED

LISTEN TO YOURSELF

I'M SCARED TO DEATH OF WHAT'S NEXT

Different than being confused or blocked, this is what happens when you face (or when you resist) change. For some of us, we are aware a change has occurred, yet we cling to the way it has always been, because it is what we know. Or you might mentally comprehend and even accept the change, but fail to acknowledge the associated emotional impact. Perhaps you are fighting change, clinging to an old behavior, pattern, person, or project that you know is not right for you — and yet, seeing beyond it terrifies you.

All of the above keeps you in a holding pattern, where you know you need to move forward but are scared. The fear becomes that of the unknown, not the actual change. Take the time to meet your fear, make friends with it, and make the fear known.

WHAT IF IT WORKS OUT EXACTLY HOW YOU WANT IT TO?

WHAT HAPPENS IF THIS DOESN'T CHANGE?

WHAT OPPORTUNITY ARE YOU WASTING RIGHT NOW?

WHERE ARE YOU SABOTAGING YOURSELF?

ARE YOU DONE YET?

WHAT DOES THE FIRST STEP LOOK LIKE?

WHAT HAPPENS IF YOUR FEAR IS TRUE?

I'M SCARED TO
DEATH OF
WHAT'S NEXT

MOVE THROUGH THE FEAR

I WANT TO FEEL GOOD

.

There isn't a human alive who does not want to feel good. Most of us are so busy being aware of all that is not going well — our fears, blocks, and pains — that we simply forget we have so much to feel good about. Even if right now you think you don't have anything to feel good about, chances are, you do.

Answer any of these questions to remind you of the power of you and the pleasure and pleasantness of your life.

WHAT GOAL(S) HAVE YOU RECENTLY ACCOMPLISHED?

WHAT DO YOU LOVE ABOUT YOURSELF?

WHAT ARE YOU THE MOST PROUD OF IN YOUR LIFE?

WHAT HAVE YOU DONE THAT HAS REQUIRED COURAGE?

WHAT DO PEOPLE COMPLIMENT YOU ON THE MOST?

WHOSE LIFE HAVE YOU IMPACTED THIS YEAR?

WHAT BRINGS YOU PEACE OF MIND?

NOTHING IS EVER MISSING

I FEEL
ALONE

You are not alone, even though sometimes you feel all alone. Sometimes life can be lonely. Sometimes it feels as if there is nowhere to turn, no one to go to, and no one on this planet who understands us. Sometimes that might be true, because after all, we are all unique. Other times we create our own loneliness. We do this by holding in or holding back, when we really want to reach out or jump in.

Loneliness can grow from a fear of vulnerability and resistance to trust. Many times we create our own isolation. There are small things you can do to take accountability for the times when you feel alone that will allow you to create deeper connections with others.

WHAT IS WORKING WELL FOR YOU RIGHT NOW?

WHAT ARE YOU WITHHOLDING?

WHAT FEELING ARE YOU RESISTING?

CAN YOU CHANGE IT?

IS IT WORTH CHANGING?

HOW DO YOU KNOW WHEN YOU'RE NOT LONELY?

DO YOU TREAT YOURSELF THE WAY YOU WANT TO
BE TREATED?

YOU ARE CONNECTED

EVERYONE ELSE HAS GONE CRAZY

You know the moment: the time when you cannot understand why people are saying what they are saying and doing what they are doing. The moment when nothing makes sense to you and if people would only listen to you, then everything would be fine, and they would not have to act, be, or do crazy things anymore. When we feel this way, odds are strong there is something we are trying to control or we think we know better than everyone else.

Perhaps you do actually know better, and if that is the case you also know that people need to learn their own lessons. Move with grace through situations when the world around you has gone mad.

WHY DOES IT MATTER?

WHO HAVE YOU BECOME?

CAN YOU LET GO OF TRYING TO BE SO SMART?

CAN YOU LET THE ANSWER BE SOMETHING OTHER

THAN YOU THINK IT SHOULD BE?

WHAT ARE YOU UNWILLING TO CHANGE?

WHERE ARE YOU IN DENIAL?

WHAT ARE YOU WITHHOLDING?

ALLOW

I CAN'T SEE MY FUTURE

How many times have you heard someone say they wish they had a crystal ball so they could see their future? If this were possible, you could receive validation that the path you are on is the right one, that your hard work will pay off, that you make a difference in the world in the way that you want to. Wouldn't that be nice? Sometimes we just want to know that everything is going to be okay, that the choices we make, the effort we put in, and the values we live by will in the end result in something wonderful.

There is no way to see the future; however, there are questions to help you generate, sculpt, and shape the vision you wish to manifest.

WHERE DO YOU WANT TO BE IN SEVEN YEARS?

WHAT WILL FREE YOU UP TO LIVE THE LIFE

YOU DESIRE?

WHAT DOES SUCCESS LOOK LIKE?

WHAT ARE YOUR CORE VALUES?

WHAT ARE YOU DOING NOW, THAT YOU DON'T
WANT TO BE DOING IN TEN YEARS?

IS HOW YOU SPEND YOUR TIME AND MONEY NOW
HELPING TO CREATE THE FUTURE YOU WANT?

WHAT IS THE LEGACY YOU WANT TO LEAVE AND
WHAT ARE YOU DOING NOW TO SUPPORT THAT?

IT'S NOT HOW YOU START,
IT'S HOW YOU FINISH

YOU DON'T ALWAYS NEED A COACH TO
WALK YOU THROUGH THE "WHAT'S NEXT" —

YOU JUST NEED A BIT OF CHUTZPAH
TO ANSWER SIMPLE QUESTIONS WITH TRUTH
AND THE WILL TO TAKE ACTION.

THE CHOICE IS YOURS

ABOUT THE AUTHOR

In 2008, Jae Ellard founded Simple Intentions, a company dedicated to developing employee awareness and publishing conscious content. In 2010, Jae authored the Mindful Life Program designed to help people disrupt patterns that cause imbalance and disengagement. To date, Jae's work has touched thousands of employees at multinational corporations in more than 50 countries spanning from Asia Pacific to Latin American, Western and Central Europe, Middle East, as well as Canada the United States. Jae has an extensive background in writing and communication with a master's degree in Communication Management from Colorado State University and a bachelor's degree in Broadcast Communication from Metropolitan State College of Denver. As a lifelong learner her passion has propelled her deep into research on human behavior, neuroscience, mindfulness, and organizational relationship systems. Jae writes columns and speaks on mindfulness in the workplace and is the author of seven books.

OTHER BOOKS BY JAE ELLARD

The Five Truths About Work-Life Balance is about the myths, misconceptions and choices available to you to create balance.

Success with Stress is about five proactive choices you can make to reduce stress.

THE MINDFUL LIFE COLLECTION

STOP & Think: Creating New Awareness is about the choices you have and the understanding of the impact of the choices you make.

STOP & See: Developing Intentional Habits is about your ability to consciously choose to create habits that support your definitions of balance and success.

STOP & Listen: Practicing Presence is about working with your choices to create deeper engagement with self, others, and your environment.

Beyond Tips & Tricks: Mindful Management is about leading groups to take accountability for making and accepting choices.

Written by Jae Ellard
Edited by Jenifer Kooiman
Designed by Hannah Wygal

ISBN-13: 978-0986238710
ISBN-10: 0986238710

The Pocket Coach, 1st edition
2015 Copyright by Simple Intentions Inc.

This book may be ordered directly through the publisher at www.simpleintentions.com.

Contact: Simple Intentions, Inc., www.simpleintentions.com.
Simple Intentions creates conscious content to generate intentional conversations.

Made in the USA
Charleston, SC
24 January 2016